AUTISM

MASKING

Helping You to Identify and Understand

AUTISM

MASKING

The truth behind the mask...

Written by Autistic Author

Emma Kendall

Contents

Acknowledgements

My sincerest thanks go to all the autistic families and people who have helped make this book possible. Together, we can provide personal insights and experiences paving the way for a better future.

Thanks to my university tutor and associated lecturers. Without your guidance, I would not have the confidence to pursue my dreams as an author.

I am eternally grateful for my family and friends. Thank you for being by my side all these years and for always providing guidance and support.

A huge thank you to my husband and my publishing team. Without you, my dream of putting my experiences onto paper would not exist.

About the Author

Emma Kendall specialises in supporting adults, children and parents of children that are diagnosed with an autism spectrum disorder (ASD).

Emma graduated from the University of Birmingham (UK) with a first-class degree in Autism: Special Education (BPhil). Her educational background also includes qualifications in Counselling, Communication and Personal Skills.

The author, Emma Kendall, was diagnosed with Asperger's syndrome in her early thirties. She comes from a family of many ASD diagnosed members, including her son.

Over the years, Emma has gained valuable knowledge and experience whilst helping families to connect and understand the complexities of the autism spectrum.

Books by Emma Kendall

Non-Fiction:

Perfectly Autistic: Post Diagnostic Support for Parents of ASD Children

Autistic Christmas: How to Prepare for an Autism Friendly Christmas

Helping You to Identify and Understand Autism Masking: The Truth Behind the Mask

Fiction:

The Adele Fox Series:

Making Sense of Love

A Different Kind of Love

Memories Full of Love

Join my Facebook page:

Emma Kendall Author

Glossary of Terms, Abbreviations and Acronyms

ADD	Attention deficit disorder
ADHD	Attention deficit hyperactivity disorder
AD	Anxiety disorder
ASC	Autism spectrum condition
ASD	Autism spectrum disorder
AS	Asperger's syndrome
Aspie	A shortened name referring to someone with Asperger's syndrome
Autie	A shortened name referring to someone with autism.
BPD	Bipolar disorder
DLA	Disability Living Allowance
DSM-V	Diagnostic and Statistical Manual of Mental Disorders (5th Edition)
EHCP	Education Health Care Plan
GP	General Practitioner
HFA	High functioning autism
ICD-10	International Classification of Diseases and Related Health Problems (10th Revision)
IEP	Individual Education Plan

LFA	Low functioning autism
Mute	Refraining from speech
NAS	National Autistic Society
NHS	National Health Service
NICE	National Institute for Clinical Excellence
Non-verbal	Not involving or using words for speech
NVQ	National Vocational Qualification
OCD	Obsessive compulsive disorder
PDA	Pathological demand avoidance
PIP	Personal Independence Payment
Pre-verbal	Words existing or occurring before speech develops
Social script/ Scripting	A written or spoken narrative used to improve the understanding of difficult to comprehend situations
Stimming	Used to describe self-stimulatory behaviour. Known as - repetitive behaviours such as hand flapping, rocking, spinning, clapping, humming, tapping
Stressor	Emotional response to the environment or emotional stimulus
Trigger	Something that causes you to respond or react in a particular way

WHO   World Health Organisation

Introduction

Why is NOW the best time to learn about autism masking?

We currently live in an age where autism spectrum disorders (ASD) are widely acknowledged and diagnosed. With the ever-increasing autism diagnosis rate, service providers, families and autistic people want to learn and understand as much as they can about ASDs to better assist and support those on the autism spectrum.

It is becoming evident that the best way to learn about ASDs is to gather autism knowledge and insights directly from autistic people.

As an author, not only am I diagnosed with an ASD, I am also a mother to an autistic son, and I hold a first-class bachelor's degree in Autism: Special Education. In addition to this, my family also includes many ASD-diagnosed members.

When it comes to understanding ASDs, there are no clear-cut explanations that can be used to define the components of this complex spectrum disorder. Each autistic individual will present their ASD characteristics differently from one person to the next because autism has many varying features.

ASDs are classified as neurodevelopmental disorders, and they are clinically characterised by impairments in the following:

Social communication and language

Social imagination and flexibility of thought

Social and emotional interaction

Restricted, repetitive patterns of behaviour

Sensory perception

In general, the core difficulties and differences presented by those on the autism spectrum are typically associated with communication and language, specifically focusing on how they socialise and interact.

If society as a whole has difficulty understanding autism communication, they may have difficulty understanding autism masking.

I was diagnosed in my early 30s. This late diagnosis resulted in many years of trials and tribulations. The main issue was that I had no idea as to why I struggled so much with socialising and connecting with people.

I look back to my childhood and think, *if I could have been diagnosed sooner, would my adult life have been different?* Communication for me has been one of my biggest struggles in life. The anxiety and stress produced by the difficulties have prevented me from doing so many things, as I knew I didn't communicate like everybody else.

I would stand and watch people, thinking, *how do you do that? Why can't I socialise like that?*

I've lost count of the many times that I've asked people, "How can you just talk to somebody and just strike up a conversation and make friends? How do you know what to say? What do you say if they respond? What if you get it wrong and they don't want to talk to you? Why don't you get anxiety when talking to new people?"

These typical social skills tend to come naturally to non-autistic people and are generally carried out without any thought or planning.

My communication barriers have prevented me from gaining employment, making friends, going to events, and so on. This has caused many mental health problems and associated disorders, ranging from bulimia (in my younger years) to suicidal thoughts, depression, loneliness and feelings of isolation. All this is what prompted me to mask my struggles.

If only I'd had somebody who could explain these differences and give me a reason as to why my brain functions differently, then I could have understood that these difficulties and differences were what made me, me. If only I had known that I wasn't broken, and I didn't need fixing; I just needed a little help with communication and an understanding of my social environment.

It wasn't until I took a course while studying counselling that I truly comprehended my areas of limitation. In that course, we focused largely on listening and body language. This brought a huge amount of awareness to my personal struggles and how I did everything differently from the other students in the course.

I learnt that the way I made eye contact was different; the way I responded to body language and social cues was not typical; I didn't process language typically; I would misinterpret many aspects of the conversations. When practising listening skills, hearing the person's distress, I felt overwhelming empathy when compared to the others. I looked at situations from different angles—ways in which the others just didn't. It was in that area of education that I realised how different I actually was because, ultimately, that course focussed intensely on language and communication.

This helped me to understand how other autistic people communicate. I began to watch and observe autistic people, and I realised they communicated just like me. I didn't feel so different after all.

This is when I recognised how much I had compensated for my differences over the years by using autism masking, and I realised the severe impact this had on me. This made me think, *if I've struggled* this *much, then how is it impacting other people on the autism spectrum?* After I finished that counselling course, I knew I wanted to help other autistic people. That's when I decided to attend university to study autism spectrum disorders.

I've always had an interest in neuro-development and studied this area largely. It was in my final year at university when I got to look into autism masking and social behaviours of autistic people. I spent the best part of the year studying and researching this area; that research was like therapy for me. I learned to understand and identify the impact society has on autistic people and how the way they connect with society as a whole can lead to success for them or disaster. The outcome typically depends on how well they can interact, and if they mask or not. And if they do mask, the masking behaviours have their own impact on the autistic person.

Researching autism taught me just how little was known about this topic, not only within the general public but in the autism professional sector also. It occurred to me, if service providers found it difficult to understand masking, then it would no doubt be difficult for many other people, autistic or not.

For that reason, I decided to put as much information and insight as I could into a book to help others with understanding this complex social behaviour.

Throughout this book, I will refer to children and adults diagnosed with an autism spectrum disorder or associated disorders as autistic, autistic people or autistic person. This is because I have found these terms to be the preferred terminology within the autism community.

I hope this book will provide you with new insight into autistic masking from my personal perspective, not just through my research but also through the experiences and knowledge I have gained throughout the years.

I want to help you understand:

> What autism masking is.
>
> How to identify autism masking behaviours.
>
> When and what triggers autism masking.
>
> Why autistic people mask.
>
> The impact masking and misdiagnosis has on autistic people.
>
> How to support somebody who masks.

I also want to finish by giving you insight into my life experiences to give you an honest look at what autism masking feels like.

Thank you for reading. I hope you enjoy the book!

Chapter 1

What is Autism Masking?

What does the term *autism masking* mean to you?

You may be a family member, partner, friend, carer or possibly a professional service provider supporting a person with a diagnosed autism spectrum disorder (ASD). You may have received an ASD diagnosis or simply just have an interest in learning about ASDs. Depending on which person you are, it will most definitely impact how you understand autism masking, and no doubt influence your own experiences.

There's no denying that autism masking is a deeply misunderstood topic, and it is typically unacknowledged within today's society. Before we delve into the details of autism masking, let's take a quick look at how much understanding and legislation has changed over the years; this may give us insight into why autism masking isn't typically recognised within society.

Back in 1943, psychiatrist and physician Dr Leo Kanner first identified the condition as *infantile autism*, which is now commonly referred to as *autism* or *autism spectrum disorder*. Kanner detected many similarities amongst the children he observed, including abnormal development and impairments in socialisation, communication and imagination. He also noted differences in intelligence.

A year later, in 1944, paediatrician Dr Hans Asperger found similarities in the children he assessed (defined as Asperger's syndrome). While he reported developmental delays and abnormalities in speech, he noted that speech was typically fluent by the age of five, and individuals showed a good level of intelligence. By the time the children reached adolescence, they typically became aware of their differences in communication and interaction when comparing themselves to their peers.

Both Kanner's and Asperger's clinical descriptions share similar core characteristics but present a wide variation of these symptoms.

It wasn't until the late 1960s, where we first saw the *Diagnostic and Statistical Manual of Mental Health Disorders, second edition* (DSM-II) (American Psychiatric Association) define autism as a *psychiatric condition*. The guide is used by clinicians and psychiatrists to diagnose psychiatric illnesses and mental health disorders. It is recognised worldwide and is typically used in the USA.

In the UK, service providers typically use *The International Statistical Classification of Diseases and Related Health Problems, tenth revision, fifth edition* (ICD-10), which is the diagnostic manual of the World Health Organisation

(WHO).

The UK also saw infantile autism being introduced to the ICD-8 in the 1960s and was continued in the 1977 revision of the ICD-9.

As research progressed, the clinical diagnostic criteria and descriptions for infantile autism were eventually identified and added to the DSM-II in 1980. This key information regarding the late classification gives us an indication as to why it's only in recent decades that we have seen an increase in clinical autism acknowledgement and understanding.

This important adjustment to legislation changed the pathway in which clinicians identified autism spectrum disorders, and with that, there was a further update in 1987 (to the DSM-III) where we saw revisions that altered the clinical description to *autistic disorder*. Additional amendments were also made to the diagnostic criteria.

In 1992, the ICD-9 was revised with additions of *childhood autism, atypical autism* and *Asperger's syndrome*, which continued in the 2013 revised edition, ICD-10. This is why we still see children and adults receiving a diagnosis of Asperger's syndrome in a number of practices across the UK and in all countries that follow this guide.

In 1994, the DSM-IV was released, which also included *Asperger's syndrome*. However, this clinical description has seen significant changes over the past few decades. This is because in 2013, when the DSM-V was implemented, Asperger's syndrome was removed and no longer diagnosed or acknowledged in clinical practice within the USA. This has caused enormous controversy within the autism community (specifically those originally diagnosed with Asperger's syndrome) regarding autistic identity and confusion and which terms should be used.

The DSM-V now categorises autism and associated conditions and disorders as a spectrum, producing a combined diagnosis of *autism spectrum disorder 1, 2 or 3.*

Level 1 – Requiring support

Level 2 – Requiring substantial support

Level 3 – Requiring very substantial support

The ICD-11 (2018) also eliminates the classification of Asperger's syndrome following that of the DSM-V, collapsing all associated developmental disorders into a single diagnosis of *autism spectrum disorder*. This is due to be fully implemented in the UK by 2022.

As a result, autism and associated autism spectrum conditions are now universally recognised as one conclusive diagnosis of *autism spectrum disorder*. This clinical diagnosis is pooling all neurodevelopmental disorders together but recognises that each person presents their ASD symptoms differently.

Not only have we seen modifications to the criteria and classification of autism spectrum disorders, but also, there have been huge advancements in recognising the differences in both male and female autistic characteristics and development.

In former times, autism was predominantly recognised as a male condition. This is because clinical evidence generally found a male to female ratio of 4:1. In recent years, the general view is that a 3:1 ratio is a more accurate figure because of missed or misdiagnosis in girls due to biased assessments. Many have suggested that girls have been turned away because assessments are geared towards spotting male autistic characteristics and interests.

In the early 2000s, we saw Professor Simon Baron-Cohen introduce a theory called the extreme male brain theory of autism, putting forward the concept that autistic brains show an exaggeration of the features associated with male brains, suggesting autistic people have an extreme cognitive style that favours systemising over empathising.

Current research suggests autistic people are not generally hyper-male, meaning autistic males don't particularly show one specific profile while autistic females show another, and there are many causal factors influencing the varied gender differences.

With that being said, research has found females to have a greater ability to adapt to their surroundings, mimicking language and actions of those around them. In addition, females also tend to have a greater need to develop connections with people and a desire to conform to social norms. However, this doesn't mean to say attaining and maintaining social interactions is well within their grasp.

Active research has shown that autistic males in general (not always) have a reduced ability to adapt in social situations when compared to females, for example, when reading social cues, responding to emotions, and so on. There has also been a recurring concept that suggests males tend to present additional behaviours such as hyperactivity, attention deficit and conduct issues.

Although we see many differences in gender, this doesn't mean there are definitive gender-specific characteristics for every autistic person. Both males and females have overlapping similarities.

The criteria currently used to assess and diagnose ASDs isn't gender-specific. We use the same principles to assess both males and females. Therefore, it is the responsibility of the assessing practitioner(s) to recognise if gender differences are present. Which, more often than not, is solely dependent on the person's experience and knowledge gained through working with autistic people.

The terms *autism masking, to mask, act* or *camouflage* are typically used to describe individuals who consciously and/or subconsciously hide their autistic behaviours and characteristics. Autistic people use masking as a means to manage the way people perceive them in social situations. Just like a spectrum, there are varying ways in which autistic people do this.

Some examples of masking include the following:

> Unnaturally performing to fit in.
>
> Mimicking social behaviour of others (e.g., facial expressions, body language, etc.).
>
> Making extra effort to make eye contact.
>
> Consciously controlling how they speak (e.g., slower, lower tone, pausing).
>
> Actively trying to reduce forms of stimming in public (e.g., to avoid drawing attention to themselves).

It could be argued that almost everybody (autistic or not) will mask daily to get by in their day-to-day lives. For example:

> A gay person may conceal their sexuality to prevent themselves from being judged, thus masking their true feelings and personal identity.
>
> When meeting new people, a person may put up a façade, masking their true personality and trying to make a good impression by portraying a faultless character.

Masking is a social behaviour; therefore, there'll be many types of masking. We know social behaviour amongst autistic people is somewhat different from that of non-autistic people. This is why those on the autism spectrum specifically mask or modify their social behaviour in relation to their autistic characteristics.

Autistic people hide their differences so they can adequately function within society. Some do it consciously throughout their lives, some just do it in certain environments or with specific people, and for some people, they won't even realise they are doing it. It just becomes an ingrained habit.

I've heard people refer to masking as 'wearing a heavy cloak.' The energy it takes to carry the social burden around all day can be exhausting.

Autism masking can also be described as a coping mechanism and is used in situations when a person is unsure of how to interact or behave. Some autistics present themselves as a different person to numerous friend groups, adapting themselves to the environment and the associated social norms. Due to this behaviour, many autistic people can be wrongly accused of having a split personality, and many have been misdiagnosed with a personality disorder.

For many autistics, masking isn't a choice. It is more of an automated response when they are uncomfortable in their environment. They try to appear like their peers on the outside: dressing the same, liking the same interests to fit in, etc. However, on the inside, they know they are different.

Many people have suggested autism masking could just be learnt behaviours. After all, it's inevitable that we will pick up learnt behaviours throughout our lives at school, home or in the workplace. But again, it's about being conscious of the *behaviours*. Autistic people have to (or try to) learn to fit in and to appease others, deterring them from their own self-identity and typical norms.

Can you imagine what it must be like to have to suppress almost every aspect of who you are? Consciously having to prepare yourself each day, just so you can socially engage? Rigorously running social scripts through your mind daily, carefully constructing all your responses and behaviours just so you can converse and interact without obvious social mishaps and judgement of your differences?

It not only becomes exhausting but also impacts you mentally, affecting confidence and self-esteem. It's not uncommon to hear autistic people questioning themselves daily, asking, "Am I good enough to be accepted in this world?"

There are many autistic people who don't feel they want or need to mask their difficulties or hide the fact that they are autistic. As we see the development of autism awareness and understanding within society, the perception and acceptance of autistic people are also evolving. In general, more and more people are actively recognising that inclusion of all differences and disabilities is a very important matter.

There are also numerous autistic people who simply can't mask. We typically see this in autistic people who have additional conditions such as intellectual or learning disabilities, mental health conditions and so on.

If we combine all the changes to legislation, social differences, gender differences and all the generic autistic intricacies together, we then see why autistic masking can be misunderstood and difficult to comprehend amongst those trying to figure out this autistic social behaviour.

Chapter 2

Signs and Symptoms of Autism Masking

There is no one-size-fits-all autism masking symptom checklist that can be used to instantly determine if a person masks their autistic characteristics or not. There are many factors that need to be considered, such as the following:

Age

Gender

Communication and language abilities/disabilities

Sensory perception

Environment (home, school, work, etc.)

Support network (friends, parents, partners, etc.)

Like an ASD diagnostic assessment, the best way to recognise symptoms is to observe and interact with the autistic person. If you are autistic and want to understand your specific characteristics, you will need to recognise how you interact socially within society.

Autism masking signs and symptoms examples:

When an autistic person relies on or uses 'scripting' to interact with people, they are masking their social difficulties. Scripting is a sequence of conversations that are mentally prepared in a person's thoughts. Scripting can also be described as 'acting out a scene in their mind,' trying to foretell how they should interact or behave in difficult situations. Of course, it's not possible to observe the social script in the mind, but we can recognise if an autistic person uses structured patterns of language for them to effectively engage with others.

Copying or mimicking other people is a common behaviour that generally starts in childhood and can follow through to adulthood. Copying is typically associated more so with autistic females, especially in their teenage years. The behaviour may be a conscious or subconscious action. They may imitate a character they see on TV, a friend, family member, and so on. They may copy the person's interests (music preferences, hobbies etc.), and how the person talks, dresses, wears their hair and make-up, and what toys or possessions the person has, and so on.

Another form of copying that is also very common in girls is to copy the most popular person (or people) in the social group. They think that if the popular person is getting it right and everybody likes them, then to get it right (or go unnoticed), copying their actions is what they need to do. The popular person can also provide a sense of safety and comfort for the autistic person.

An autistic person may constantly change their image ('which mask should I wear today?'). In doing so, they may have developed a lack of self-identity caused by years of masking. This may have led to a misunderstanding of who they are, which can result in not having a sense of self or purpose.

Masking can occur if an autistic person's support network is disrupted, for example, if a familiar teacher is changed or removed from an autistic child's class. If that child has had to act in a certain manner or mask when in that teacher's presence to build a connection or to fit in, when the new teacher takes over, the autistic child will have to start all over again. They will try to find out which 'character they need to play' so they can connect and feel comfortable interacting.

An autistic person may consciously avoid social contact because they know they struggle in social environments. At school or work, they may prefer to sit on their own at break times or walk around, trying to find alternative things to do just so they can pass time. Keeping themselves occupied masks their anxiety and difficulties of not knowing how to interact effectively.

Many autistic people have difficulties with expressing or reciprocating typical social emotions and behaviours. They may have to mask this by conforming to expected social behaviours; for example, if an autistic child has an aversion to being touched, they may not like it when their parent(s) tries to cuddle or kiss them. But, because this social interaction meets the emotional needs of the parent, the child unavoidably responds to their parent's social demand. The child may appear awkward or unnatural in their response when cuddling; this is when they use the mask to hide their discomfort.

An autistic child may appear withdrawn, wanting to 'slip under the radar.' This allows them to refrain from drawing attention to themselves, enabling them to avoid social communication and interaction. They may prefer to *cling* to a familiar adult (teacher) to help them to feel *safe*. In this comfort state, the child can then effectively communicate. The child may go from one extreme to the other, from not wanting to chat within their peer group to then chattering constantly with their familiar adult and not wanting to stop talking.

When an autistic person has social difficulties, they may mask this by being the 'quiet one in the group.' They tend to prefer to sit and analyse and observe everything around them. When they are comfortable or when they are with people with whom they can let their 'mask drop', a completely different character may appear. This behaviour is typically referred to as a 'chameleon', because the autistic person changes behaviours, personality, expressions etc., to suit their environment.

They may develop a school or a work 'persona', adapting their personality and behaviours accordingly. People may pick up on the obvious distinctions in behavioural and personality changes. For example, a teacher may notice that a child has a particular class where they act like the class clown, being disruptive and rude, yet when they are put in a different class (a different social environment), they become the prize pupil, settled with no issues.

Autistic adults may depend on an alcoholic drink to be sociable and to attend events they wouldn't usually have the interpersonal skills for. They use alcohol as a coping strategy to relax and mask their anxiety or inability to naturally interact like a non-autistic person.

If you are a parent to an autistic child, you may notice your child dropping the mask when around familiar people, but as soon as they are in an environment that is out of their comfort zone or control, the mask goes back on, even if you are around. This can be difficult for parents when one day the child has carried out an activity with no issues, but the next, because the social environment has changed, that mask goes back on, the behaviour changes and they no longer do that activity.

An autistic child or adult who flitters from one social group to another may do this because they have difficulty maintaining social connections because they simply can't keep up the mask. Friends may tire of the autistic person's constant differences in behaviour (failing to maintain the mask) and reject them.

When a child or adult typically does well at school or in their workplace with no issues, but then explodes into disruptive meltdowns or raging anger once home in their 'safe space', it is a huge sign that they have been masking for the duration of the day. The energy it takes to mask and 'fit in' can be mentally and physically exhausting.

This could also have the opposite effect: they may be very loud, obnoxious and unruly at school or work but perfectly fine with their comforts at home, where they can chill and relax.

A mask can also provoke a tendency to 'live a lie.' They may change themselves and make up imaginary stories, friends, events, etc., just so they can fit in. This can develop into a habit, and they may acquire a name for themselves as being a prolific liar. People may refer to the behaviour as 'living in a fantasy world.' Some autistic people are very good at carrying this mask; however, many just don't have the social ability to keep it up, and this is where it causes many issues for them.

How an autistic person uses and presents their masking symptoms will undoubtedly vary from one person to the next. The duration of the masking behaviours will also vary and change over time with development, coping strategies, and a better understanding of their needs and why they mask.

Ultimately, the most important thing to remember is, just because they may look okay on the outside does not mean to say they are okay on the inside.

Chapter 3

When and Why Autism Masking is Used

To better understand when and why autism masking is used, it is important to speak directly to the autistic person at hand. They are the only person who will know why they truly mask and to what extent it is relied on. Additionally, we must never assume that we can know everything regarding an autistic person's particular social differences and difficulties.

Through my own experiences of autism masking and the knowledge gained through talking to other ASD diagnosed individuals, I have found that masking typically develops in childhood, particularly the teenage years.

Masking is typically triggered when social demands exceed an autistic person's limits, such as in the following cases:

When they realise they are not like their peers and struggle to fit in.

When experiencing pressure to appear 'normal.'

After suffering from continuous bullying from peers, teachers, employers, etc.

When high expectations are placed on them from family members, expecting them to appear and behave in a certain way.

In circumstances when they are misunderstood.

If they experience big changes, a new environment, new people, etc.

When pressured into liking similar interests as peers (instead of liking their unique interests).

When they don't want to be singled out.

They may recognise in themselves that they are socially different/inept (may feel embarrassed about showing their true self).

When they are subjected to social/information overload.

When they struggle to make eye contact, or recognise body language and social cues, or have difficulty understanding jokes and idioms.

When they don't know how to express their own characteristics 'appropriately' in social settings.

They may be fascinated with non-autistic 'social norms', analysing and observing the way non-autistic peers interact and communicate, wanting to learn how to do it themselves.

When being criticised, you're too loud, too quiet, too fidgety, too unapproachable, etc, always having their characteristics picked at.

When they are unsure of how to act or behave.

Some just think that masking is what everyone does, and they don't know anything different.

The teenage years can be difficult for both autistic and non-autistic people. It's in these maturing years when it's essential for autistic children to develop their social and emotional cognisance. Meaning, they need to develop many skills such as social skills, flexible thinking, working memory, self-control, emotional and behavioural regulation, decision making, problem-solving, and many more. It's in these moments when an autistic person typically gains self-awareness of their areas of limitations, social differences and difficulties.

These are the typical developmental skills and characteristics that tend to present numerous difficulties for those on the autism spectrum. This is due to autistic neurodevelopmental differences in language, communication, executive functioning and flexibility of thought.

The mask innately becomes a natural response to hide any differences and difficulties they endure. If the autistic person is masking their difficulties to compensate for their struggles, then people supporting or assessing them will only see a masked child, teenager or adult. This could become problematic for those wanting ASD support and assessments.

The autistic youths who haven't experienced issues when integrating and adapting socially in school may find difficulties arise when transitioning to adulthood where independence is more prominent in their daily functioning, for example, when going to college, university or the workplace, or when seeking relationships and friendships.

Typically, when youths transition to adulthood, parents are expected to take a step back and allow their child to support themselves. The social demands become much more personal for the autistic person when they no longer have their parents to advocate or to step in when assisting with their social connections. This is where we see the social aspect that triggers the behaviours of autism masking.

The social difficulties and differences typically trigger autism masking in the following situations:

> Socialising with people they do not know well (failing to develop a social connection).
> Making new friends.
> Socialising with extended family members.
> Interacting with professionals, such as teachers, employers, doctors, etc.
> Shopping (engaging with staff).
> Using public transport.

Autism masking allows people on the spectrum to hide their differences, making it easier for them to integrate into society, allowing for fewer complications and stress. It prevents bullying, judgement and stereotyping, helping them to feel accepted.

Masking also helps to hide autistic behaviours that are generally recognised within society as inappropriate or weird; one behaviour, in particular, is stimming. If a person, for example, is hand flapping, making vocal tics/sounds, rocking or tapping, this will undoubtedly grab people's attention. This is where people who are disturbed by the stimming behaviours stare or make a judgement. Suppressing stimming behaviours when around others can take enormous effort, which may have major consequences for the autistic person. This once again is another factor that can create potential mental health issues or impact an autistic person's well-being.

The mask also acts as a coping strategy when anxieties are in a heightened state, by creating stability and control when they are feeling uneasy and dysfunctional. It also assists with predictability, for example, when anticipating social events, how to act, behave, interact, etc., (they can practice social scripts prior to the event).

Masking can naturally be triggered when wanting to search for a companion. For many autistic adults, without the mask, they would have had major difficulties when pursuing or forming a relationship with a love interest.

This is because of the emotions, anxieties and social demands that are involved when building a connection and getting to know somebody intimately. The mask may be very useful when used in these circumstances; however, it can also create a negative response. For example, if a person was to mask for the first six months of a relationship but then changed character when they felt comfortable, this could impact the social connection that had formerly developed, hindering the relationship. The love interest may become confused by the autistic person's behaviour, making statements such as, 'You've changed 'or, 'Why can't you be the person I met six months ago?'

Autistic people don't tend to feel the need to mask when they are with people they know well, such as parents and partners; they tend to relax and be themselves. These interactions are valuable when needing to recuperate and to be able to comfortably be themselves, but again, this is where behavioural changes are prominent and could cause difficulties (mental health issues). This is because the sense of self-identity can become conflicted when switching in and out of masked behaviours.

A common consensus that reverberates amongst autistic adults is, when autistic people are around other autistic people, the need to mask is significantly reduced. This is because of the following:

> They feel more accepted.
>
> They don't have to hide and can be themselves.
>
> They can be themselves without judgement.
>
> They feel safe with other autistic people.
>
> They have consideration for each other's needs.

However, those who have masked for many years can still find it very difficult to entirely 'drop the mask' around other autistic people because of it becoming an inherent habit.

Another major factor that triggers masking is the motivation to experience a greater quality of life. In these circumstances, the positive aspects that can be achieved from masking include the following:

Acquiring and maintaining employment effectively.

Developing successful relationships.

Functioning adequately as a parent.

Feeling normal and accepted.

Having a sense of purpose and a feeling of belonging.

Over the years, when I have spoken to autistic adults regarding why and when their masking behaviours started, many were able to pinpoint a certain situation. They recalled their feelings and thoughts, the circumstances and the triggers, and all the relevant details that forced them to continually alter their social behaviour(s).

This leads us to the question, why is this common autistic social behaviour overlooked?

A consensus view seems to be that if autistic people know they are doing it, then why isn't this common knowledge across all clinical and professional service providers, including medical staff, teachers, support workers, carers, and so on?

Equally, if service providers are inexperienced in the subject, then how are family members of autistic children meant to learn and understand it if they have no awareness or information regarding this behaviour? We know this could have a potential long-term impact on a child's experiences and quality of life.

Yes, we do have greater awareness and understanding of autism spectrum disorders, but many aspects are overlooked surrounding ASDs, not just autism masking.

We also need to teach acceptance. As a society, we are unavoidably pressured to act and behave in a certain way to be socially accepted, but it's important to remember (and accept) that people ARE different, and it's OK to be different.

Chapter 4

Impact of Autism Masking

As previously explained, autism masking isn't a social behaviour that people on the autism spectrum typically choose to do; it is a fundamental social tool that is adapted accordingly to assist them in their day-to-day functioning. This ultimately enables autistic people to socialise and gain greater connections within society.

Whether it's conscious or subconscious, this social behaviour can provoke many questions surrounding the impact masking may have on an autistic person's quality of life.

People may assume that if masking is an inherently social tool that allows them to adapt socially, then that autistic person will function adequately for life, with long-lasting positive outcomes.

I'm sure you'll agree that's very unlikely, and it will most definitely be subjective to each autistic person.

Unsurprisingly, one of the most common aspects that continuously appeared when studying autism masking was the severity of the impact produced over time, from actively keeping up the mask.

Yes, it may produce a greater quality of life with positive results, but it's the aftermath that generates countless repercussions regarding self-identity.

As mentioned earlier, masking changes many aspects of a person's personality. The mental aspect required, and the incessant energy it takes to keep up these changes can lead to long-term mental health issues and detrimental effects on a person's well-being.

When talking to autistic adults, almost all of them shared details on how masking impacted their mental health negatively. The common negative effects resulted in the following:

Depression

Anxiety

Low self-esteem

Increased suicidal ideation

Nervous breakdowns

Tiredness, burnout or exhaustion

Many stated that masking prevented friends and family from understanding or accepting their ASD diagnosis, which led to further negative effects, such as the following:

> Family and friends not comprehending their daily complexities of ASD.
>
> Missing out on crucial support.
>
> Almost always having feelings of loneliness.
>
> Having to continuously adjust themselves to fit in.
>
> Not effectively communicating their feelings.
>
> Always feeling like a failure.
>
> Being regularly misunderstood.
>
> Feeling like they are faking their autism spectrum disorder.

From both personal experience and knowledge acquired since supporting people on the autism spectrum, the most common detrimental aspect of masking is the difficulties autistic people have when family and friends will not accept or acknowledge their ASD diagnosis. Many family members will be in denial and refuse to discuss anything relating to ASDs, thinking the autistic person is just making a fuss or trying to bring attention to themselves.

It's common to hear autistic people being accused of 'acting autistic' by family and friends. This is because they have spent years trying their hardest to hide their difficulties, but when they can no longer keep up the mask, people pick up on the difference and don't take their ASD diagnosis seriously. All these negative reactions can be very damaging for the autistic individual and can exacerbate feelings of not belonging.

Many people in society struggle to grasp the concept that an autistic person can go to college, work, get married, have a family, be intelligent, be successful, and maintain friendships and relationships. What these people are not understanding is the effort it takes for autistic people to do this, and the coping strategies that are put in place to enable them to live effectively, not realising the detrimental impact from years of keeping up this 'social persona' can have on them mentally, physically and emotionally. This is why we see so many autistic adults with severe mental health issues.

The implications significantly influence an autistic person's character and state of mind, which is why we also see various co-morbid conditions and disorders associated with ASDs, such as the following:

Anxiety disorders

Self-harm

Eating disorders

Sleep disorders

Behavioural disorders

Personality disorders

Depression

Addiction/obsessive disorders

Autistic meltdowns, anger issues and violent/aggressive behaviours can also develop, or existing destructive conditions can become exacerbated due to the continuous masking. This will no doubt impact conduct at school, work or relationships, and it may trigger additional catastrophic coping strategies, such as the following:

Illegal drug and/or prescription drug use

Alcohol dependency

Food addictions

Shopping/hoarding compulsions

The impact may also affect relationships with friends and family, for example, becoming withdrawn and distant, unmotivated to join in with friends or family events, not wanting to leave the house, faking illnesses so they can avoid socialising, and losing interest in favourite hobbies, tv shows, music, and so on.

They may appear aloof, spending lots of time lost in their thoughts. It may trigger relentless over-thinking, scrutinising all the details of their daily interactions.

> *Did I say this right? Did I interpret the situation wrong? Why don't they like me? How can I do it better next time?*

The mask itself may create disastrous consequences, for example:

An autistic person may copy social behaviours but have no true understanding of them or why people do them.

They may become extremely invested in looking

the part and fitting in. The social behaviour can become obsessive and end up costing a lot of money whilst trying to get it just right. For example, a girl trying to fit-in and keep up with the current trends may be highly focussed on the 'perfect' clothes, hair and nails, and not realise or care about the financial burden of keeping up this image.

Following the popular person (or a group) may not always be the best choice. It could get them into trouble if they copy immoral and unlawful behaviours, or if they are put into social situations for which they just don't have the interpersonal skills. This could be seen as a weakness and an opportunity to manipulate the autistic person's behaviours and actions. In these circumstances, an autistic child or youth (or even an adult) may be foolishly coerced. This is why having an understanding of what autism masking is when supporting them is important, so they don't put themselves in vulnerable situations.

Autistic people may enjoy socialising and seek social connections but become unaware of the impact it has on them whilst sustaining these relationships. 'Social burnout' is a common term used within the autism community due to the effort it takes to maintain and manage a social life. Becoming overwhelmed and exhausted is a regular after-effect.

Many people on the autism spectrum are highly intellectual and academically skilled. This can give people a false perception of their abilities, which can result in them appearing as if they aren't struggling or having difficulties. This is another reason why so many autistic people go unnoticed or 'slip under the radar.'

Autistic people may have difficulty with keeping or maintaining a job, or a child may change schools often. This can be due to many reasons, such as not being able to be themselves, or not being able to mask effectively. Not understanding important social cues and behaviours can cause enormous anxiety and stress, resulting in the feelings of 'get me out of here!' The only way to feel safe is to walk away from the setting, meaning they'll have to start all over again in a new environment. If coping measures aren't put in place, this can become a repetitive cycle that is difficult to break.

Many children and adults miss out on essential support in school or in the workplace; they place so much effort on being invisible, so people don't see their true difficulties. The problem being, the mask helps them to appear fine and capable.

Masking can impact others, such as family members. If they are dependent on an autistic person to maintain a job or run a household, masking may be relied upon much more and become too much to maintain. If an autistic person doesn't have the mental capacity to maintain this mask, the dependency and expectations placed on them by others can trigger many negative associated mental health issues.

Masking can be very stress-inducing, which can make it difficult to concentrate when given specific tasks to complete. For example, in the workplace, this may cause further worry about what is happening next and about what is expected of them. Another example, if a child is asked to tidy their bedroom, stress can make it difficult when trying to multi-task or when trying to figure out where to start or how to complete a task.

As mentioned before, suicidal thoughts can become a daily occurrence when struggling to keep up the mask. They may think they can't do it anymore, and suicide is the only way to get out of their complex life.

Complex communication barriers such as miscommunication and misunderstanding combined with the lack of support within families can lead to autistic people being estranged from many of their family members and friends.

Masking can induce eating disorders. This can be caused by many reasons, such as the following:

Constant feelings of anxiety may cause them to have headaches, feel sick, or have a tightened feeling in their throat, which may make food difficult to eat.

If the autistic person already has sensory difficulties with food, this may heighten or trigger issues.

Having control over their food may give them a sense of control over their life; this may become a (negative) coping strategy for them.

They may become obsessive about particular food groups, colours, tastes, textures, etc.; again, this could be caused by a need for control or a sensory aspect.

Overeating may become an issue. This could be due to many factors, such as using food as a comfort (coping strategy). Food can also provide fulfilment through stimulating the brain (activating 'happy hormones'), e.g., sugary foods. A common expression used in society is 'eating too much can put you in a *food coma.*' They don't specifically go into a coma, but the food makes the body feel sluggish and tired but at the same time relaxed, calmed and content. Like many food compulsions, this can create a 'natural high.' This feeling can become addictive, resulting in patterns of overeating. This could also trigger binge-eating, bulimia, and many other associated eating impulses.

If masking was better understood and recognised in general, then maybe we could help autistic people reduce their negative experiences and after-effects.

Instead of trying to 'fix' or change an autistic person, maybe society could just try to understand and empathise a little more.

In doing so, we could potentially reduce suicide rates, unhealthy addictions, prescription drug dependency, mental health conditions, loneliness, and so on.

After all, as a collective, humans are innately wired to want to feel connections and love. Just because autistic people are *wired differently*, doesn't mean to say they can't gain access and have the opportunities to experience and achieve an enjoyable life.

Chapter 5

Misdiagnosis

♦

A frequent recurring issue that is common amongst those on the autism spectrum is late diagnosis and misdiagnosis.

Once again, why do we continue to see these recurring issues?

Especially in a time where we are witnessing tremendous improvements in medical practice, and we have a much better understanding of ASDs on the whole. The advancement of research has demonstrated this, but when it comes to identifying ASDs, it seems to still present many complex issues.

With that in mind, let's take a look at what the existing medical literature says. Focussing on both the *DSM-V* (2013) (as mentioned in chapter one), and the clinical guidelines put forward by the *National Institute for Clinical Excellence (NICE) (The Health Foundation, 2018)*. This is an independent organisation, typically used by the National

Health Service (NHS) in the UK.

The particular NICE guideline we will look at is: *Autism Spectrum Disorder in Under 19s: Recognition, Referral and Diagnosis (2011).*

Both guides provide specific diagnostic criteria for ASD, and both share similar brief autism masking statements. A summary of both guides:

> *When assessing for ASD, autistic characteristics must be present. However, clinicians are to be aware that autistic characteristics may not present initially or may not fully manifest until social demands or existing support mechanisms exceed the autistic person's limits. Clinicians also need to recognise that autistic characteristics may become masked by learnt strategies later in life.*

The information provided by the guides successfully acknowledge autism masking; however, no details or explanations suggest how to identify autism masking.

On viewing the NICE guidelines for adults: *Autism: Recognition, Referral, Diagnosis and Management of Adults on the Autism Spectrum (NICE, 2012).*

Autism masking is mentioned on numerous occasions, alerting clinicians to recognise masking behaviours, but once again, with no explanations on how to do so.

Could this be one of the contributing factors as to why we see countless members of society being wrongly diagnosed or undiagnosed?

To give a startling indication of my experiences with misdiagnosis, over sixty per cent of autistic adults I have questioned stated they were initially incorrectly diagnosed. The common misdiagnosis included the following:

Personality disorder

Bipolar disorder

Depression

Anxiety disorder

In addition to receiving a misdiagnosis, many had been subjected to inaccurate observations by clinicians, stating they didn't initially receive a diagnosis due to comments such as the following:

You can't be autistic; you can make eye contact.

You are too empathetic and caring.

You can maintain and join in the conversation.

You are just a bit odd.

You are just rude.

You would not be able to parent if you were autistic.

You would not be able to maintain a job.

Depression was generally the main misdiagnosis

followed by an anxiety disorder. Does this suggest that current diagnostic criteria and clinical training methods are misunderstanding this complex social behaviour?

Late diagnosis or misdiagnosis can also result in a person being prescribed the wrong medicine, or they may have missed out on crucial medication.

Other areas of support that are incredibly helpful for autistic people and typically missed out on are the following:

Counselling

Cognitive behavioural therapy

Speech and language therapy

Executive functioning assistance

Help and understanding in the workplace

Education health care plans (EHCP), and individual education plans (IEP) in school

Funding, e.g., personal independent payments (PIP)/disability living allowance (DLA)

A common notion repeated profusely within the adult autism community is, they would like to have been diagnosed as early as possible so they could have gained a greater understanding of their difficulties and differences. This would have allowed them to gain adequate support and therapies if needed.

As previously mentioned in chapter one, the clinical descriptions of ASDs and Asperger's syndrome weren't clearly defined until the 1980s and then updated again in the 1990s. This needs to be taken into consideration for the high number of people under-diagnosed within the adult and senior population.

Typically, diagnosis for children and youths is now on the rise due to greater awareness, government and private funding, and research, which is continuously progressing within the professional sector.

Autistic adults, parents of autistic children, support workers, etc., are equally bringing greater awareness to society through their personal experiences and development.

With this much-anticipated progress, maybe in the not so distant future, we will possibly see this generation gap in ASD diagnosis greatly reduced.

In doing so, we must not forget that this is a spectrum disorder, and we most definitely need to view the autistic symptoms with this in mind.

I think it's fair to say, if you have a lack of autism understanding and knowledge, then you're not going to fully understand autism masking.

We also need to remember there are many false stereotypes associated with ASDs.

Some examples of stereotypes include the following:

> *Autism is only seen in non-verbal, low-functioning people.*
>
> *If you don't 'look' autistic, then you can't possibly be autistic.*
>
> *The absence of typical autistic characteristics equals only very mild autism.*
>
> *If you can function day-to-day, then you don't need support.*
>
> *It's predominantly a young boy's condition.*

Stereotyping could be another huge factor influencing the reasons why masking has gone unnoticed, and to put it simply, masking behaviours don't fit the typical autistic stereotype.

Could this be contributing to why females are typically missed or misdiagnosed? Is it because they do actually have a greater ability to mask?

I often hear of girls being accused of 'pretending to have social difficulties.' This is because in the correct environment, many autistic girls can communicate exceptionally well, but put them in a compromised situation, and they tend to crumble when under pressure.

They are not 'pretending' to have difficulties just to be awkward or disruptive; they just don't have the ability to continuously conform socially. This is another important fact that we need to remember: masking and pretending are two completely different autistic behaviours.

It is very common to see adults and parents of autistic children actively seeking diagnosis when they are no longer coping and have hit rock bottom (so to speak). This is when they realise they just can't cope, so they seek help.

Often, people don't typically know how to describe why they aren't coping, because there are numerous contributing factors. Generally, they know something is different, but they can't quite grasp what. Again, this can often be associated with masking, and it most likely contributes to why professionals struggle to understand or recognise what symptoms are being presented in front of them.

The differences in communication also present many challenges. Many autistics will tell you they have the words in their head, but they get stuck and don't want to come out or they come out differently than what they meant.

This is another contributing factor as to why we see a large number of autistic adults working independently or as self-employed. This is because the medical system and employment sector have regularly failed to meet their needs. Working for themselves takes away the stress of being bullied, stereotyped, misjudged and misunderstood.

Working independently also allows them to 'drop the mask.' This is another reason why school-aged children don't like working in groups and why they work much better on their own. Many autistics say, once they have found their comfortable environment to work in, they can completely drop the mask, and they say it's the best feeling in the world. No pressure, no anxieties, no worries. They may lose acquaintances, but many say it much outweighs the benefits to work by themselves.

Another major issue with misdiagnosis or late diagnosis is missed opportunities to gain appropriate support and therapies, particularly in the form of counselling. As we know, many autistic children and adults typically struggle with mental health disorders at some stage in their lives. The diagnosis would give a clearer understanding as to why a person has certain difficulties and what is causing them.

With that said, counsellors also need to be experienced in recognising masking behaviours to be able to accurately support autistic people. We are slowly seeing an increase in specialised ASD counsellors, but they are still few and far between, with long waiting lists.

There is also an increase in people seeking private ASD assessments as an alternative route for diagnosis, rather than the conventional services such as the NHS. Many reasons are contributing to this, such as the following:

> They've failed to get an ASD referral for an assessment from relevant services, such as GP, a health visitor, and so on.

Government-funded providers tend to have longer waiting lists for assessments.

Unqualified and qualified inexperienced service providers haven't followed legislation; therefore, they are not referring people accurately. Subsequently, they prefer to make their own assumptions when deciding if a child or adult requires a referral or assessment.

An adult or parent of the child does not agree with the outcome of the final assessment result and would like a second opinion.

Service providers, for example, teachers or a family member, may refuse to provide specific information regarding the person seeking a diagnosis, e.g., written evidence that assists the generic referral and assessment process. This is often because the teacher or family doesn't acknowledge or recognise the autistic symptoms in the individual.

Commonly, they don't know how to provide written evidence, or they simply just turn a blind eye to the situation caused by their inexperience.

Once again, this all coincides with the identification and understanding of ASDs. If a service provider has limited knowledge and experience when supporting those on the spectrum (especially in the ASD referral process), then undoubtedly, the individual will go undiagnosed and be left to their own devices with no support or alternative care.

Chapter 6

Providing Support

When supporting an autistic person (whether they mask or not), it's important to take the time to observe and listen to them. Learn from that person what their ASD characteristics are, and in what ways (if any) being autistic impacts them.

You may already have a clear understanding of their differences, abilities, difficulties and areas of limitation, but if you don't, it would benefit you greatly if you could gain a clearer understanding by identifying areas, such as the following:

> Do they experience any sensory difficulties and triggers?
>
> What are their routines and repetitive behaviours?
>
> What are their coping strategies?
>
> Do you understand their level of communication and use of language?

How do you connect with them?

Can they self-regulate their emotions and behaviours?

Do they have a special interest?

What are their stimming behaviours?

What makes them happy or sad?

What impact does the autistic individual have on you?

Notes:

_____

_____

_____

_____

_____

_____

_____

_____

_____

_____

_____

_____

Just like any relationship, to make it work, you need to understand each other and have a connection. If you are supporting a pre-verbal or non-verbal person, this won't be relevant as masking won't typically be an issue. But for those who do have spoken language skills and rely on masking to interact, building trust and familiarity is very important when communicating and interacting sociably.

It'll also require you to be clear in your spoken language and to explain what your intentions are when supporting them. This way they don't have to try and figure you out and mask their own behaviours in the process.

If you are a family member or close with the autistic individual, they'll most likely drop the mask around you; however, this will mainly depend on what connection you have with them. Is it a loving or volatile relationship? Is there trust between you? Do you understand their ASD characteristics? Is that person dependent on you? Do you communicate effectively with each other?

There will be many contributing factors to consider, but just recognise that their masking behaviours will no doubt be different with you when compared to a service provider. If the person doesn't mask and you don't see any masking behaviours, it's still important to gain a clear understanding of your child's (or adult) autistic characteristics so you can help them if they do experience social difficulties in the future.

Key areas to focus on:

Identify their social areas of difficulty.

Are there any specific triggers for masking (e.g., they struggle to talk in group settings, can't express true feelings, etc.)?

Does the person rely on social scripts and/or predictable language to communicate (e.g. resort to talking about special interests when having difficulty making conversation)?

Does the person choose to avoid specific interactions?

Do certain social demands trigger behaviour changes?

Which social environments trigger masking?

Does the person mimic other people and their actions?

Does the person rely on a 'social persona' to get by daily?

Do they want help? If so, what kind?

Notes:

Another important point to remember is that each and every autistic person will present their masking characteristics differently from one person to the next. Some may have an outstanding vocabulary but have difficulty interacting. Some may interact amazingly well but not recognise social expressions, such as sarcasm or humour, and so on.

Other key areas to focus on:

> Does their social (e.g., school/work) environment need adjusting? For example, do they need extra breaks if suffering from social overload, anxiety or stress?

> Recognise if they are being bullied or experiencing damaging criticism from others. Do they need help with learning how to respond or deal with the situation? Do they have the social capacity to emotionally and mentally support themselves?

> To get an idea of the true extent in which the mask is relied upon, observe the person in different settings with different interactions.

Notes:

Providing support:

> Show compassion for their differences and difficulties.
>
> Don't judge, criticise, or make assumptions about their abilities and limitations.
>
> Don't force or tell them how to behave, act, or engage in situations where they don't have the interpersonal skills to do so.
>
> Allow them to use stimming if and when they need to.
>
> Don't place unrealistic expectations on them with the hopes of 'getting everything just right.'
>
> Don't actively encourage masking; allow them to show their personality, interests, etc.
>
> Help them to understand the importance of self-love.
>
> Make them comfortable to be themselves; allow them to be who they want to be.
>
> Guide them with their social skills if they experience social mishaps.
>
> Assist or help them with personal interactions if need be (provide a social script, explain what to do in tricky situations).
>
> Discuss typical social rules and etiquette, so they have an awareness of appropriate social behaviours that are commonly used within society.

Help them so they can socialise and interact effectively for them. Don't force them or expect them to understand or use typical social skills because this isn't an autistic person's 'typical' way to communicate. For example, if the person struggles to understand the dynamics when talking in groups and prefers one-to-one communication, allow them to stay quiet. Don't force them to interact when the group is actively talking amongst each other.

When everyone has stopped talking, allow the autistic person to ask questions one-to-one within the group if need be; don't automatically assume they can apply typical social skills.

Always remember to question how they are using masking as a social tool and what impact it is having on them.

If you are autistic, it is important to recognise if, how, why and when you mask. This is vital when distinguishing if the masking behaviour is impacting you or not.

How to do this:

Recognise your behaviour changes; how and why do you change?

Identify your social areas of difficulty (do you recognise body language, social cues, sarcasm?).

Recognise if you have communication differences (e.g., need extra processing time, misinterpret situations, struggle to keep up with the conversation, and so on).

Do you have difficulty making friends or maintaining friendships?

Understand how you impact others when socialising (e.g., do you zone in and out, shut down, need space, talk too much, forget to pause or let the other person speak, become aggressive in your speech, and so on?).

Do you want to fit-in? If so, does fitting-in take great effort to maintain?

Are you having an identity crisis?

Do you rely on special interests to interact?

Do you feel listened to?

Do you put barriers up and block people from connecting with you?

Do you live in your mind, overthinking things, repeating the scenarios in your thoughts?

How many people know the 'unmasked' you?

Notes:

_____

_____

_____

_____

_____

_____

_____

_____

_____

_____

_____

_____

_____

_____

Impact:

Do you appear confident on the outside but feel like you're screaming on the inside?

Are you prone to being bullied? Do you get verbally or emotionally attacked?

Do you get overwhelmed easily?

Is anxiety an issue? Does it prevent you from socialising?

Do people believe in your diagnosis?

Do you need time to recover after social events, outings, etc.?

Do you get manipulated into uncompromising situations due to your social differences (e.g., being taken advantage of or experience mental, physical, domestic or sexual abuse, and so on)?

Do you have mental health problems?

Do you receive adequate support (counselling, financial support, and so on)?

Do you have any negative coping strategies? What are your coping strategies?

Notes:

_____

_____

Most importantly, do you know what being autistic means specifically for you? This may sound like a silly question, but how can you understand your personality traits and connect sociably (allowing yourself to drop the mask) if you don't even know what your autistic characteristics are?

If you need to learn, you could do so by listening to other autistic people. There are lots of autistic advocates on YouTube who share their life experiences and offer guidance. If you want to connect, there are many adult Facebook groups, bloggers and advocates on Twitter who allow you to discuss things online.

If you don't like using social media and prefer to meet up with people, the National Autistic Society (NAS) holds many support groups all over the UK. Their details are on their website, www.autism.org.uk.

I've found, our autistic differences aren't overly distinctive when you are with the 'right' people. Self-awareness of our differences can help us to find those 'right' people. For me, this has helped others (and myself) to understand and accept my differences.

I have autistic and non-autistic friends whom I have known for many years. They accept me for being me, Emma. I don't focus on my label (ASD), and I don't let it be a barrier in this complex fault-finding society. If I am having difficulties when talking to new people, I have learnt to initially say, "I'm shy; it takes me a little while to open up." This is what works for me and stops me from appearing rude. They don't need to know I'm neurologically wired differently; they just need to know what I struggle with in conversation, and I find, most people understand what 'shy' means when compared to the word 'autism.' In chapter seven, I will go into greater detail, explaining my communication and masking behaviours and difficulties.

You just find what works for you and your area of limitation, and experiment. It takes practice and confidence; something that doesn't typically come naturally to us will no doubt be challenging. Try to slowly push your barriers if they are stopping you. Be proud of yourself. Acknowledge your achievements, even if nobody else does.

We can't rely on others to always provide positive feedback. We need to learn how to let our mind be our best friend. Teach your mind to say positive things like, *"I am great. I can do this. Today I am going to give it a try. I may be different, but I am a unique kind of different."*

Learning how to love yourself and be your mind's best friend can be the best medicine when improving self-esteem and confidence. This is a complex world that we live in, and you can only do your best. Learning how to be kind to yourself within your mind will benefit you greatly.

If you mask, and it works for you without any repercussions, then you do what you need to do to meet your own needs.

Chapter 7

My Personal Experiences: Being Autistic and Autism Masking

School.

I am what I guess you would call a 'textbook' diagnosed girl with Asperger's syndrome. This is because I meet Dr Hans Asperger's criteria, especially the communication aspect. I have always been a very shy, introverted person with little confidence and low self-esteem.

Throughout preschool and primary school, I had one best friend. That friendship was very poignant and central as to why I coped so well and 'went under the radar.' That singular focused friendship meant I could play happily in my own little bubble with that person, and we provided great support for each other. That friendship continued through to high school.

After the first few years at high school, I began to venture out from that 'best friend bubble' and included myself in a group of girls (those girls would agree, we were what you would call the odd girls, the misfits, the outsiders because we didn't get included within the popular groups). My best friend was still there, but the co-dependency of that relationship wasn't as prominent.

I remember copying the other girls. I was the girl who followed the popular girl in the group.

Copying the same interests and the same clothes, I tried my best to fit in. It was never about wanting everyone to like me or wanting to be the popular person myself. I just wanted to feel included and to join in with all the teenage fun.

This friendship circle came easy for me because the girls shared the same 'special interests' (boybands). We all dressed the same and collected the same merchandise, and listened to the same songs. It was a very happy time in my childhood, and they provided that feeling of belonging.

But they were my only friends. In my last years of high school, our classes were split up, and I no longer had them for support whilst in class. Because I didn't have the typical social skills to just make conversation with the person sitting next to me or with those around me, I stayed very quiet and shy and kept to myself.

This is where the masking behaviours started. I really felt the impact of not being able to effectively connect or communicate in these circumstances.

These familiar friendships that had kept me invisible and helped my struggles to go unnoticed were now gone. My struggles were in full view. This triggered tremendous anxiety, and my school work suffered. I would fake being ill just so I could avoid the lessons that made me feel uncomfortable. There were many times when I didn't need to fake it because it genuinely did make me feel ill.

It was like my whole world of communication had flipped upside down because I didn't have any idea of how to cope in these circumstances.

Another aspect that significantly impacted me at school was when I had to stand up and speak in front of people. I know this can be stressful for most people, not just autistic people, but what I will never forget is the severity of the stress-induced behaviours. My whole body would feel like it was violently shaking, yet if you were to look at me, you wouldn't see the movements. I would have to force my voice out, whilst at the same time try to control this explosion that was going on in my mind. I would suffer horrendous fear of getting it wrong. As I stood up there, with everyone staring back at me, I couldn't hide behind my friends; I was up there all on my own. I felt violated, as if people were coming into my intimate personal space, having my struggles and difficulties with communication laid bare for all to see.

There were times when I could internalise and hide my many difficulties on the inside, but it was my body language that truly exposed my difficulties.

One of the main distressing memories that I have of my childhood is, I had a tendency to go bright red when experiencing communication difficulties. Especially when I was with those whom I didn't know very well (and being a dark-haired, pale-skinned, freckled northern lass, it didn't help matters when wanting to hide my bright-red, blushing face).

It's like I knew when it was going to happen; I could feel it. In my mind, I would be saying to myself, *Please don't go red, please don't go red…*

But I couldn't stop it. It felt like my mind knew how to only do things this way. I couldn't change this anxiety process that my body and mind would go through when forcing myself to connect. Yet, I knew I had to endure it so I could fit in and not get bullied. The struggles I experienced in doing this impacted me enormously.

If I could have had one wish back then, I would have asked for this struggle to stop. Instead, I had this obvious clear sign that showed everyone that I was socially inept. They saw my social incompetence when communicating, and I knew it.

It got so bad that at one point, I just naturally started to go into mute mode. Inside, I would get so stressed, it was like my brain was responding by saying, *Nope, I'm not gonna let you get stressed like that anymore, so I'm gonna switch your communication off so you don't have to talk to anyone.*

But that exacerbated matters even more, because I shut myself off and became this weird, shy kid who would watch from the sidelines, wishing she could join in.

Later on, in my teens, my friends started having boyfriends. At this stage, there was a lot of peer pressure to have a boyfriend too. The idea of having a boyfriend was really exciting for me, someone to connect with and hang out with, but the reality of getting a boyfriend just baffled me.

There was this one time when a really popular guy whom all the girls liked asked me to be his girlfriend. To this day, I remember the wave of confusion that rushed over me. Like the other girls, I quite liked this guy, but I had no idea if he was joking, or being serious, or if I'd even heard him correctly. It was like my brain couldn't comprehend what he had said. My poor self-esteem and lack of confidence, combined with my inept social skills, made this situation one that was way beyond my abilities. I went bright red and completely mute; I couldn't respond, not one word. He must have thought I was really odd when I walked away. Afterwards, all I could think of was, why had he asked me when there were all these perfect girls? Why would he want a weird, broken girl like me?

To this day, I still don't know if he was serious or not. I couldn't read his body language or recognise if it was sarcasm. I'll never know if he was mocking me or not.

Academically, I did ok. I was an average pupil. I think what held me back from doing better was my tendency to zone out when the teacher was expecting us to focus or retain large amounts of information. All my school reports always said the same thing: *If Emma spent as much time on her work as she did staring into space, she'd be an A* pupil.*

Being in my dreamworld was my coping strategy whilst in school. Shutting off from all these expectations placed on me by my teachers helped me feel calm, so I could stop stressing about the things that I needed to remember.

Another academic aspect of school that I found difficult was mathematics and information technology (IT). To this very day, I struggle with simple equations. The only way I can explain how my brain sees numbers is, it's like learning a new language. Numbers are foreign to me; it's like my brain gets stuck with each component of the mathematical question. I am the same with IT and computers. My brain cannot retain simple actions like cut and paste, how to save a file, and so on. Something that is super simple to most people creates huge complications in my brain.

As an adult, I now realise I have autistic comorbid conditions called *dyscalculia*, combined with a form of *dyslexia* relating to computers and how I read the information. Now that I understand this, I know I need to write everything down regarding computer actions that I need to perform daily to help me use a computer when writing my books. Thankfully, my husband is naturally gifted in mathematics and computers, and he teaches me and provides this area of support.

Employment.

On leaving school, I was fortunate enough to gain an apprenticeship in catering and hospitality. This provided a structured job that gave me routine and predictability. I thoroughly enjoyed being creative with food and providing a service for others. This occupation lasted for ten years (between the ages of 16 and 26).

Just like school, I was quite reserved and was very naïve when mixing with the other employees. I would cling to familiar people, and I observed their social behaviours intensely. In the beginning, I worked with some really good people, and there were a lot of opportunities for me to work independently in my own department. As time went on, when I was required to integrate within the team, I had difficulty with all the different personalities.

It was very different compared to school, and the interactions were out of my depth; I got them wrong quite frequently. This made me an easy target and vulnerable in situations where I needed to show competence in my work.

I began to 'follow' the crowd, learn their interests, and learn social scripts that I could use with certain people to prevent awkward silences (again, I often got this wrong). There was one particular guy whom I worked with (one-to-one); I had to learn from him to acquire my NVQ qualification. He was about ten years older than me; he was a nice, quiet, timid, calm person with a friendly nature. He was very good at his job and easy to work with and learn from, but because I had difficulty connecting with him and struggled to work him out, I didn't know how to make conversation with him. All I could do was ask questions regarding our cooking. In this situation, I felt like the 'chameleon.' I could talk to other members of staff but not with this one guy, the one guy I needed to spend a lot of time with. It was like my brain would freeze, and it became very awkward and uncomfortable for me because I just didn't know how to make small talk. I felt like the weirdo, and I really noticed my social incompetence in this situation. When I think of how I felt, it deeply affected me that I couldn't get this one thing right. I would scream at myself in my head, *Talk! Just say anything that comes to mind!*

But my mind would draw up a blank. The struggles when interacting in these types of situations still pose a difficulty, and this is why I now work independently for myself (writing books). It takes away the stress of the social aspect that comes with working in a busy company with lots of staff.

It was during that catering job when I suffered tremendous anxiety and depression; this triggered a lot of mental health conditions. I felt like that school girl again, silenced by my inability to fit-in, connect and communicate effectively. These issues resulted in failed friendships and the inability to further my career. I was also restricted because of my failure to utilise communication to manage staff or to be a team leader.

I placed way too many expectations on myself to be like the other employees whilst trying to naturally integrate in this particular social environment. Many times, I would hand my notice in, then withdraw it repeatedly, because I was scared of the change. After all, it was all I had known since the age of sixteen. When I turned 26, I finally broke down and decided to escape this difficult social environment.

I walked away from my familiar. I didn't have a clue where to start. It was then that I realised I had no choice but to master the art of job interviews if I was to be employed again.

Over the years, I have communicated well in interviews, and 90% of the time I got the job I'd applied for. I think the fact that it was usually one-to-one communication allowed me to compose myself (because there aren't too many people involved). I am also very literal in my answers; I gave honest responses and didn't come across as being fake or desperate. I would also practice my social scripts prior to the interview and have all the relevant questions and answers prepared beforehand.

Like most people who attend interviews (autistic and non-autistics), anxiety can be a big issue. But because I had had lots of experience with controlling all the feelings associated with anxiety (since childhood), I had become much better at controlling my body language, such as going bright red or appearing very nervous. By this time, I had built a mask that enabled me to perform well in this type of environment. Being good at interviews helped me to get the job, but once I started the employment phase, I found I didn't typically have the required interpersonal skills to keep up the job requirements. Because of this, I flittered from job to job.

First, I worked at a dog-boarding kennel as a dog handler. I loved working with the animals, but once again, I didn't connect or fit in with the staff. I was either taken advantage of and given all the undesirable shifts that nobody else wanted (like weekends and bank holidays), or I was given the dirty, strenuous jobs.

Next, I worked at a solicitor's firm as a conveyancing secretary. That job only lasted four weeks because I couldn't come to grips with the computer or connect with the other employees. It was a closed-in small office, where everyone worked in amongst each other. It was an intense environment, and I found there was too much of a sense of hierarchy amongst the staff; it was an awful experience. Everyone had this huge sense of self-importance; I couldn't bear it. Every day, I felt like I was being suffocated by their egos. It was a very surreal environment, something I could never adjust to. One day, I just stood up from my computer desk, peered over at everyone and said, "I'm off. I'm done with working here. It's not for me. Bye!" I grabbed my belongings, and off I went. I can still feel that sense of relief that whooshed over me as I walked out the door.

Then I got a job at a doctor's surgery as a receptionist. Let's just say, I was way too blunt and literal in my speech for this position. I didn't have the patience or interpersonal skills when dealing with the public. Even when I tried to mask my differences in social skills, I would struggle. Thankfully, I was put on paperwork duties quite often. I think the manager realised this was much better suited for me. Once again, I left because of my inability to keep up with the social aspect of this job. The daily interactions became too overwhelming and exhausting. I suffered social burnout quite frequently whilst in this environment.

Then I got a barista job in a Costa coffee shop. I was quickly promoted to supervisor. Little did I know my incompetence in maths would cause enormous issues. I had to deal with cash, stock checks, staff hours, etc. I don't know what I was thinking when I applied for this job. I was constantly involved with the customers and the staff. It was very full-on. I was amazing at training the staff and implementing health and safety procedures and great at promoting brand standards. I had all the skills to work there, but I failed at positioning myself as a team leader in a managerial position. I really couldn't grasp this responsibility or how to run a shift with numerous staff members.

It wasn't until my late twenties and early thirties that I recognised patterns. All these jobs required me to work with the public or within a closed environment closely with people. Clearly, it wasn't working for me and was impacting my mental health catastrophically. The amount of effort I placed on applying specific masks to particular situations just became too much to deal with any longer.

It wasn't long before I realised I needed help. This is when I was referred for an ASD assessment and diagnosed with Asperger's syndrome.

I spent a while looking back at my life. I finally had answers to all my difficulties. I began learning everything I could relating to the subject. This is when something just clicked, and I decided to be serious about what I wanted in life. That's when I decided to go back into gaining an education, which has now resulted in my specialised subjects (autism and supporting those on the autism spectrum).

Mental health.

My mental health issues began to take a hold of me in my late teens. The main contributing factor to my difficulties was that I knew I was different. I hated the fact that I couldn't communicate like my peers and was impacted tremendously from trying to keep up the mask whilst trying to fit in. It just became too much for me.

I started to fall into a state of self-destruction. I attacked everything about myself because I couldn't find anything to love about me. Then, one day, I just cracked. I started to punish myself by making myself sick after meals. Being sick and purging my food was never about wanting to lose weight or look a certain way. I was already very slim and didn't have any weight to lose. It was more about my feelings.

Every time I was sick, I was purging the hatred feelings

too. This became a coping strategy, albeit a negative one, but something within those moments kept me from losing my mind. It somehow gave me a break from my inner demons. This lasted around six months. I became painfully thin, and people around me were starting to notice; this led to me getting help.

I was referred to counselling. I had many sessions, and over time, the purging stopped. However, the way I felt about myself hadn't changed. I still felt very alienated in this world and placed a huge amount of pressure on myself to socialise, make friends and find a boyfriend to somehow connect with someone.

The counsellor didn't help my inner feelings. She treated me as though I was just attention-seeking, like I was making up all my difficulties. She didn't take me seriously, so I couldn't connect with her. Maybe it's because I masked very well in those sessions? Maybe that's why she thought I was pretending and wasting her time? Over the years, I have seen many counsellors. Not once did I find one who truly understood and empathised with my differences and difficulties. If it wasn't for the counselling course that I attended, I don't think I would have managed as well as I do now.

In my early twenties, I dipped even lower. I had experienced a few failed attempts at keeping a boyfriend. I thought I would be on my own forever. The feelings of loneliness were the most intense emotions that engulfed me. I felt completely trapped in my isolated little world. I remember getting to a stage where I just wanted to end everything. Everything became such an effort. This social persona that I tried to maintain had failed miserably. All it did was exacerbate my negative feelings about myself. At the time, I was very close with one of my brothers, and my grandma had always been my best friend. I spent hours talking on the phone to them. They pulled me out of my isolated world and gave me a sense of belonging. My brother is very funny and knew how to make me laugh and smile; we had a beautiful connection. Both of us relied on each other in times when we both needed emotional support. This emotional support helped me a lot and pulled me out of my dark space. I started to be kinder to myself.

In the times when I looked after my mental health, I began to feel like my true self. I would do the things that I enjoyed. I stopped following the crowd and focussed on doing things that made me happy. It was in this state of self-love that I let my barriers down and found a special connection. That special connection was my future husband.

There was something about him. I just knew he wasn't like the other guys I had dated. We clicked. I didn't feel the need to mask; communication came easy, and for once, I could be me. And if you're wondering if he is on the spectrum, my husband isn't clinically diagnosed, but he does fit the criteria for Asperger's syndrome. He doesn't need a diagnosis; all we know is we understand each other very well, and we bring balance to each other's lives. I have never had to mask around him, never. I understand his difficulties and areas of limitation, and he does mine. He doesn't like crowded places, certain noises, etc. These things trigger him instantly. When he is triggered, I can empathise with his inner feelings and know not to exacerbate them but to calm him. We have many situations like this where we support each other.

Sixteen years later (and two children in tow), we are still very much each other's best friend. We provide stability for each other, just like I used to get from my first best friend all those years ago.

Having a husband who understands me has been a crucial part in maintaining healthy mental health. I still have all those communication difficulties when connecting with others, but I've learnt to accept my differences.

I don't live by my diagnosis and let it hold me back. I've just had to learn how to adapt and recognise when I need to put the mask on and take it off instead of constantly trying to maintain this social behaviour.

It has taken a lot of work regarding self-love and recognising my needs to get to this stage where I am very happy within myself, and have healthy mental health. All my experiences have taught me to never judge a person's difficulties, and to never assume that you can just say a magic word and make everything better.

When you have endured years of difficulties, it will take time and effort to learn about those difficulties and to understand how you can make things easier for yourself.

In my case, I just need someone to connect with me and to understand me.

For others, they will no doubt have very different circumstances than me and have had completely different situations.

This is why I always say, get to know the autistic person and understand their autistic characteristics. Never assume you can completely understand all their difficulties. Be there to guide them and offer support, listen and respect their needs, don't try to 'fix' them.

Learn to accept their differences and try to empathise with them.

In doing so, you'll understand,

...the truth behind the mask.

Thanks for reading!

Amazon reviews are extremely helpful for authors.

Please add a review on Amazon and let me know what you thought. Thank you.

Emma xxx

Also available from Emma Kendall

Perfectly Autistic
Post Diagnostic Support for Parents of ASD Children

This helpful book covers areas, including:
ASD terminology.
Helping your child understand their ASD diagnosis.
Helping your child how to explain to others they are
diagnosed with an ASD.
Teaching your child how to advocate their needs.
Calming and coping strategies.
Autistic behaviours.
Emotional connections and self-confidence.
And much, much more.

Adele Fox Series Book One

Making Sense of Love

Autistic… single… and not quite sure how to mingle.

As Adele Fox approaches thirty—being single is her normal. Would she like a boyfriend? Yes. Does she know how to date? Not exactly.

Making small talk, flirting, reading body language, understanding jokes and sarcasm—sounds easy right? That is unless you have a communication difference.

When a chance encounter brings Adele together with a charming travel agent, she finds herself being whisked away for a romantic Valentine's weekend. Little does she know, her world is about to be turned upside down.

Adele Fox Series Book Two

A Different Kind of Love

Autistic... In love... And ready to start the next chapter in her life.

Not only has Adele Fox found her dream man, she's also found a new home, a new job and a host of other dilemmas to go with it.

When Adele's differences complicate matters with her new work colleagues, she takes a trip back to her familiar life in London, when an old flame from her past unexpectedly returns, throwing her life into a spin, which leads her to question:

Was the huge life change worth it? Was it the right decision? Is she capable of being loved?

Adele Fox Series Book Three

Memories Full of Love

Autistic… newly married… and trying to fit into a new family.

As Adele Fox enters married life as Mrs Beeton, not only does she have to adjust to becoming a wife, she also has to form a relationship with her husband's parents.

Whilst on their honeymoon, Adele unexpectedly finds out about a Beeton family secret that has been kept hidden and buried for years.

Little does she know, what she says, and what she hides will have consequences and could ruin her marriage.

Does Adele ruin her relationship with her new family? Will she overcome and reveal her own secret?

Also available from Emma Kendall

Autistic Christmas
How to Prepare for an Autism Friendly Christmas

Being a parent to a child on the autism spectrum can be challenging at the best of times, but when you add a very busy season to the mix, full of confusing Christmas traditions, visual changes, social events, and disruptions to routine, it can become even trickier. Whether you're making plans to visit family and friends, or having a quiet peaceful Christmas at home, there will be many preparations that need to be considered.

Order direct from Amazon